Automated, objective texture segmentation of multibeam echosounder data - Seafloor survey and substrate maps from James Island to Ozette Lake, Washington Outer Coast

Steven S. Intelmann[1], George R. Cutter[2], and Jonathan D. Beaudoin[3]

[1]Olympic Coast National Marine Sanctuary, NOAA
[2]Southwest Fisheries Science Center, NOAA
[3]Ocean Mapping Group, University of New Brunswick

U.S. Department of Commerce
Carlos M. Gutierrez, Secretary

National Oceanic and Atmospheric Administration
VADM Conrad C. Lautenbacher, Jr. (USN-ret.)
Under Secretary of Commerce for Oceans and Atmosphere

National Ocean Service
John H. Dunnigan, Assistant Administrator

National Marine Sanctuary Program
Daniel J. Basta, Director

Silver Spring, Maryland
November 2007

DISCLAIMER

Report content does not necessarily reflect the views and policies of the National Marine Sanctuary Program or the National Oceanic and Atmospheric Administration, nor does the mention of trade names or commercial products constitute endorsement or recommendation for use.

REPORT AVAILABILITY

Electronic copies of this report are available from the National Marine Sanctuary Program web site at *www.sanctuaries.nos.noaa.gov*. Hard copies are available from the following address:

National Oceanic and Atmospheric Administration
National Marine Sanctuary Program
SSMC4, N/ORM62
1305 East-West Highway
Silver Spring, MD 20910

COVER

NOAAS Rainier survey launch.

SUGGESTED CITATION

Intelmann, S.S., G.R. Cutter, J.D. Beaudoin 2007. Automated, objective texture segmentation of multibeam echosounder data - Seafloor survey and substrate maps from James Island to Ozette Lake, Washington Outer Coast. Marine Sanctuaries Conservation Series MSD-07-05. U.S. Department of Commerce, National Oceanic and Atmospheric Administration, National Marine Sanctuary Program, Silver Spring, MD. 31 pp.

CONTACT

Steven S. Intelmann
Habitat Mapping Specialist
NOAA/National Marine Sanctuary Program
N/ORM 6X26
2725 Montlake Blvd East
Seattle, WA 98112
(206) 861-7603
steve.intelmann@noaa.gov

ABSTRACT

Without knowledge of basic seafloor characteristics, the ability to address any number of critical marine and/or coastal management issues is diminished. For example, management and conservation of essential fish habitat (EFH), a requirement mandated by federally guided fishery management plans (FMPs), requires among other things a description of habitats for federally managed species. Although the list of attributes important to habitat are numerous, the ability to efficiently and effectively describe many, and especially at the scales required, does not exist with the tools currently available. However, several characteristics of seafloor morphology are readily obtainable at multiple scales and can serve as useful descriptors of habitat. Recent advancements in acoustic technology, such as multibeam echosounding (MBES), can provide remote indication of surficial sediment properties such as texture, hardness, or roughness, and further permit highly detailed renderings of seafloor morphology. With acoustic-based surveys providing a relatively efficient method for data acquisition, there exists a need for efficient and reproducible automated segmentation routines to process the data. Using MBES data collected by the Olympic Coast National Marine Sanctuary (OCNMS), and through a contracted seafloor survey, we expanded on the techniques of Cutter et al. (2003) to describe an objective repeatable process that uses parameterized local Fourier histogram (LFH) texture features to automate segmentation of surficial sediments from acoustic imagery using a maximum likelihood decision rule. Sonar signatures and classification performance were evaluated using video imagery obtained from a towed camera sled. Segmented raster images were converted to polygon features and attributed using a hierarchical deep-water marine benthic classification scheme (Greene et al. 1999) for use in a geographical information system (GIS).

KEY WORDS

Benthic, habitat mapping, sediment classification, multibeam echosounder, local Fourier histogram texture features, essential fish habitat, Olympic Coast National Marine Sanctuary

TABLE OF CONTENTS

Topic	Page
Abstract and Key Words	i
Table of Contents	ii
List of Figures and Tables	iii
Introduction	1
Survey Area	2
Sonar Acquisition and Data Logging	3
Sonar Data Processing	3
Image Classification	4
Groundtruthing	7
Discussion of Survey Results and Interpretation	8
Acknowledgments	17
References	17
Appendix 1. Vessel Offsets	21
Appendix 2. Bathymetry Surface	28
Appendix 3. Backscatter Imagery	29

LIST OF FIGURES AND TABLES

Figure/Table Number and Title	Page

Figure 1. Extent of 2002 (green) and 2003 (red) MBES survey effort near Lapush, WA 2

Figure 2. Backscatter mosaic showing areas of void data along nadir tracks. Segmentation with LFH method using xyz data. Segmentation of backscatter using entropy and homogeneity derivatives. 4

Figure 3. Schematic of data layers input into the Spatial Analyst maximum likelihood classification procedure. 6

Figure 4. Location of groundtruthing validation in relation to individual survey blocks.. 7

Table 1. Survey effort statistics for HMPR-110-2002-04.................................... 8

Table 2. Distribution of bottom hardness for each sonar mosaic classified from survey HMPR-110-2002-04... 8

Figure 5. Seafloor substrate polygons, Ozette Lake to Carroll Island with bottom_id codes taken from Greene et al. (1999)................................... 9

Figure 6. Seafloor substrate polygons, Carroll Island to Cake Rock with bottom_id codes taken from Greene et al. (1999)................................... 10

Figure 7. Seafloor substrate polygons, Cake Rock to James Island with bottom_id codes taken from Greene et al. (1999)................................... 11

Figure 8. Example of homogenous bathymetry and unique backscatter signature as segmented by the modified LFH procedure. 12

Figure 9. Example of data layers to the maximum likelihood classification routine (except C) with resulting segmentation output (C).. 13

Figure 10. Clipped section of area110_0204b, illustrating a geomorphic representation of seafloor substrates produced through the segmentation of acoustic MBES data. 14

Figure 11. Example of rock features near Hand Rock and Cape Johnson............. 15

Figure 12. Example of refraction artifact encountered in the 2002 survey data..... 16

Table 3. Frequency of sound velocity casts acquired each day during the 2002 and 2003 surveys.. 17

INTRODUCTION

In response to congressional amendments of the Magnuson-Stevens Fisheries Conservation Act, all fishery management plans (FMPs) are required to describe and identify essential fish habitat (EFH) for their respective fisheries (Public Law 104-297). As FMPs can encompass regions as expansive as the entire Pacific Coast, addressing this mandate requires highly efficient methods for describing and characterizing various habitat attributes. Notably, the composition and texture of surficial sediments is widely recognized as being an important element of EFH, and plays a major role in determining the distribution and abundance of many groundfish species (Carlson and Straty 1981; Love et al. 1991; Stein et al. 1992; Krieger 1993; McConnaughey and Smith 2000).

Recent advancements in acoustic technology, such as multibeam echosounding (MBES), can provide remote indication of surficial sediment properties and further permit highly detailed renderings of seafloor morphology across broad scales and in relatively short time as compared to traditional grab or core sampling. As such, MBES data-based seafloor maps have gained broad acceptance for providing a means to segment seafloors (Mayer et al. 1999; Todd et al. 1999; Kostylev et al. 2001; Dartnell and Gardner 2004), populate hierarchical marine classification schemes (Greene et al. 1999; Alee et al. 2000; Harney et al. 2006), and hold promise for informing the EFH designation process.

With acoustic-based surveys providing a relatively efficient method for data acquisition, there exists a need for efficient and reproducible automated segmentation routines to process the data. Other work has described techniques using local Fourier histogram features (Cutter et al. 2003), grey-scale covariance texture indices (Cochrane and Lafferty 2002; Intelmann et al. 2006) and various statistical derivatives (Harney et al. 2006) to quantitatively segment acoustic seafloor imagery, yet these techniques vary in degree of reproducibility, robustness, and processing autonomy.

Using MBES data collected by the Olympic Coast National Marine Sanctuary (OCNMS), and through a contracted seafloor survey, we expanded on the techniques of Cutter et al. (2003) to describe an objective repeatable process that uses parameterized local Fourier histogram texture features to automate segmentation of surficial sediments from multiple types of acoustic imagery with a maximum likelihood decision rule. Video from a towed camera sled was integrated with sedimentary samples, backscatter, and the bathymetry data to describe geological and biological (where possible) aspects of habitat. Using a hierarchical deep-water marine benthic classification scheme (Greene et al. 1999), we then created and attributed polygon features for use in a geographical information system (GIS). The report provides a description of the mapping and groundtruthing efforts, and technique and results of the automated segmentation procedure for each area surveyed in 2002 and 2003.

SURVEY AREA

In 2002 and 2003 respectively, approximately 42 km^2 and 49 km^2 of MBES-based seafloor mapping was conducted from the mouth of the Quileute River near Lapush to roughly Sand Point near Ozette Lake (Figure 1). Survey records were obtained from July 27 – August 02 in 2002, and August 28 – September 25 of 2003. Water depths ranged between 0.5 and 35 meters throughout the survey area.

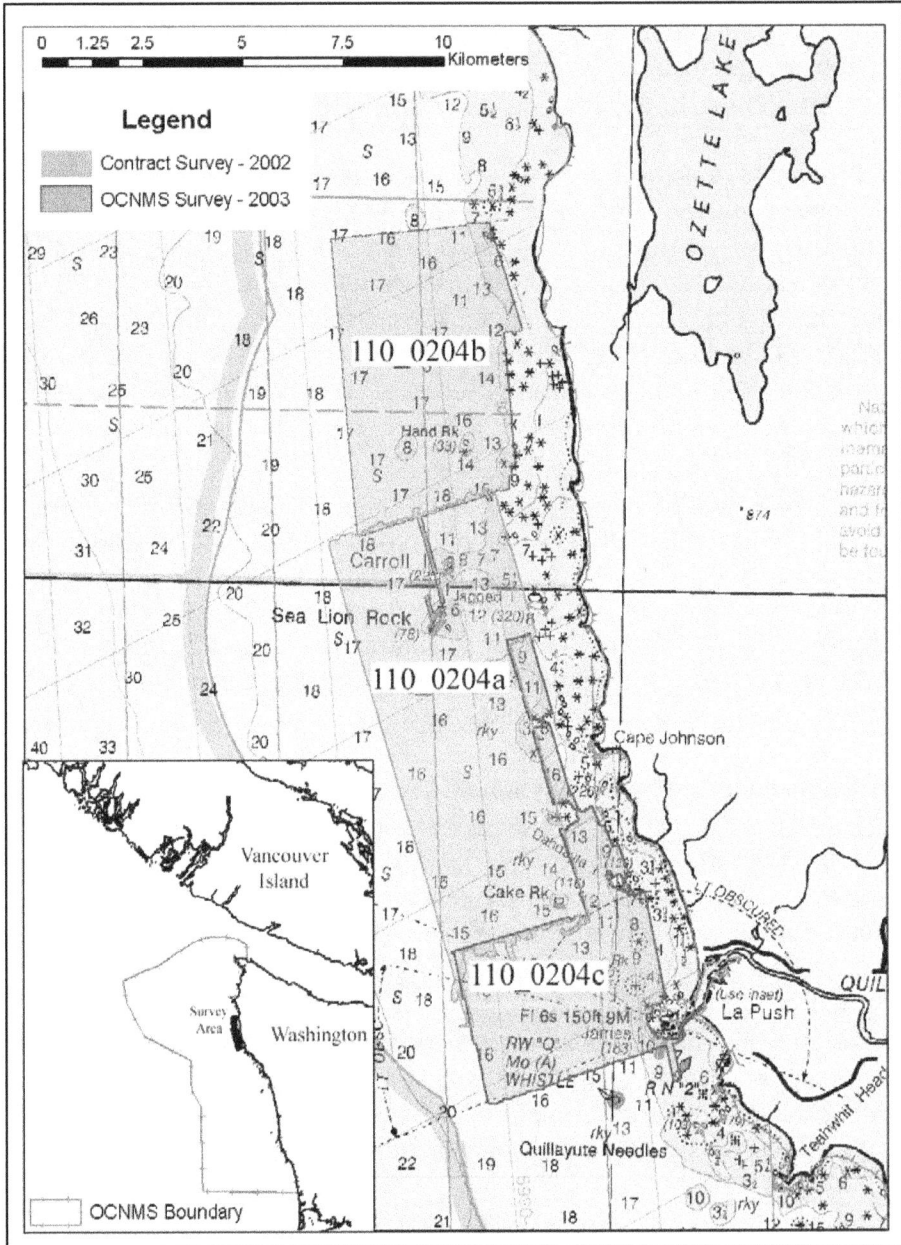

Figure 1. Extent of 2002 (green) and 2003 (red) MBES survey effort near Lapush, WA. The survey was divided into 3 blocks (110_0204a, 110_0204b, and 110_0204c) to reduce file size and to accommodate more efficient data archival and sharing. Large-scale inset provides context placement along the Washington coastline and within the Sanctuary boundary.

2

SONAR ACQUISITION AND DATA LOGGING

The 2002 contract survey, awarded to the Seafloor Mapping Lab at California State University Monterey Bay (CSUMB), used the 9.8 m *R/V MacGinitie* as an acquisition platform while a 9.8 m survey launch provided by the *NOAA Ship Rainier*, and operated by OCNMS, was used to acquire the 2003 data. A Reson 8101 MBES with extended range projector was used on both vessels. The echosounder was hull-mounted on a retractable flange for the 2003 survey but pole-mounted to the bow on the *R/V MacGinitie*. Vessel speed was targeted at 8 knots during acquisition. Sensor offsets and photos for each vessel are provided in Appendix 1.

Sonar data were logged in Extended Triton Format (XTF) using Isis Sonar (Triton Imaging International) with the "Full-New" side scan beam forming technique, a process that yields less noisy output by combining the bathymetry beams into two side scan beams where adjacent pairs of beams are then averaged and the brightest points of the averaged beams are then ultimately used (Reson 2003). Vessel attitude and positioning for each of the launches was monitored with a TSS (Applanix) POS/MV 320 and logged in Isis Sonar. Survey line control was accomplished through differential GPS (DGPS) using Hypack marine positioning and surveying software with sound velocity corrections being made through use of Seabird SBE 19plus CTD profilers. Water level observations were acquired from the Neah Bay tidal station 9443090 and applied with zoned corrections.

SONAR DATA PROCESSING

Bathymetry data were cleaned of anomalies using Caris HIPS software, creating BASE (Bathymetry Associated with Statistical Error) surfaces for each of the three main survey blocks with the CUBE (Combined Uncertainty Bathymetric Estimator) method (Calder and Mayer 2003). A 5x5 surface interpolation with 12 nearest neighbors was used to fill small data gaps. Accepted xyz values from the interpolated CUBE surface were converted to Arcview ascii grid format at 1-meter resolution using WGS84 UTM zone 10 projection parameters.

For best use in seafloor characterization, sonar echo strength data should be normalized to leave only the seafloor's backscattering strength as the sole source of signal strength variation. Because commercial software packages currently available for processing acoustic backscatter perform only a rudimentary geo-registration through use of a flat seafloor assumption and additionally ignore variations in acoustic source level and receiver gain, production of acoustic backscatter imagery was accomplished using software tools developed by the Ocean Mapping Group (OMG), University of New Brunswick (Beaudoin et al. 2002). Three separate mosaics were created for each survey block from the RI_Theta, side scan, and snippet packets. However, only the side scan data was used in the classification process since the 2002 survey platform was not snippet enabled. The side scan backscatter imagery was mosaicked at 1-meter resolution and exported to Arcview ascii grid format.

IMAGE CLASSIFICATION

To date, OCNMS has used textural derivatives (i.e. homogeneity and entropy calculated from either multibeam backscatter or side scan sonar data) and applied a supervised image classification using a maximum likelihood decision rule to segment acoustic data into discrete substrate types (Intelmann and Cochrane 2006a, Intelmann et al. 2006, Intelmann and Cochrane 2006b, and Intelmann et al. 2007). Although this method provided objective results, substantial manual subjective editing was required to clean up poorly classified regions, such as near-nadir (Figure 2, black areas visible throughout inset C).

A segmentation routine previously described by Cutter et al. (2003) offered an alternative method of autonomously classifying acoustic data using local Fourier histogram texture features, and relied solely on using bathymetry data to segment the imagery (Figure 2, inset B). Contrary to backscatter imagery, calculating textural indices from bathymetry data avoids problems associated with classifying the near-nadir backscatter artifacts (shown in Figure 2, inset A) since there can be continuous data coverage along nadir.

However, in cases where roughness of the seafloor is uniform (i.e. uniformly flat or with identical textural pattern at all spatial scales), statistical roughness or textural properties calculated from bathymetry data may not discriminate between facies. However, backscatter intensities in these areas sometimes indicate a unique acoustic signature. In other words, if the seafloor consists of flat mud or flat rock the bathymetry will

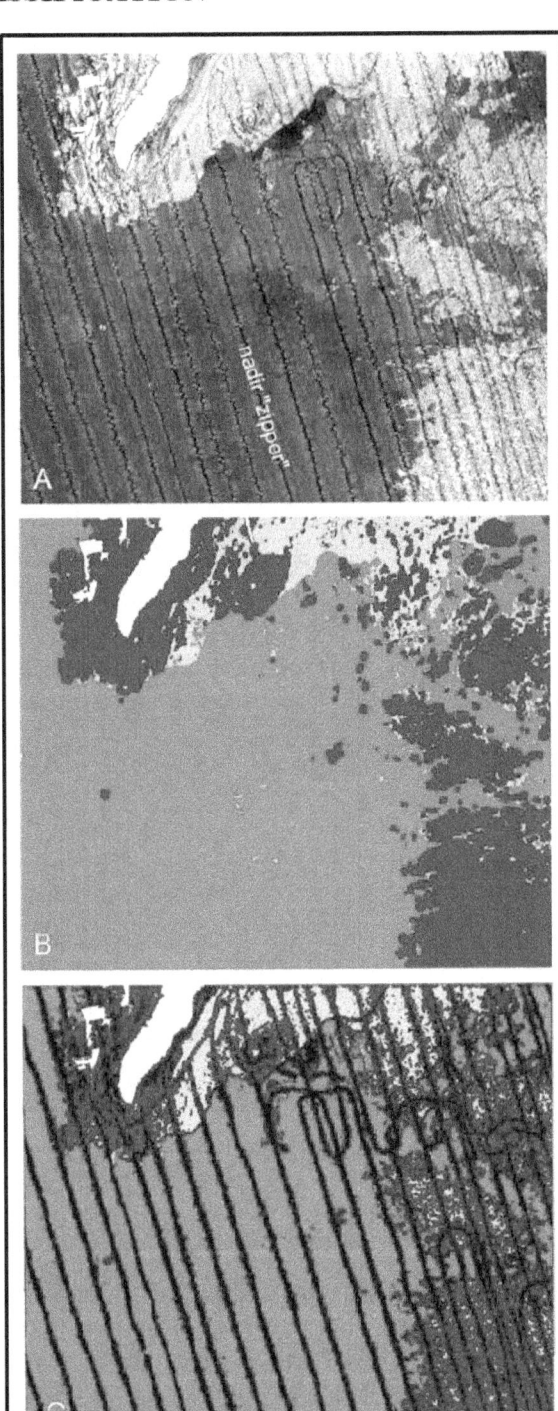

Legend
nadir   soft   mixed   hard

Figure 2. Backscatter mosaic showing areas of void data along nadir tracks (A). Segmentation with LFH method using xyz data (B). Segmentation of backscatter using entropy and homogeneity derivatives (C). Note nadir misclassification in C.

4

not indicate a difference and texture features or roughness measures do not provide enough information to differentiate bottom type in these cases. Through describing local spatial variation of grid cell values, we tried incorporating backscatter intensity into a segmentation rule along with LFH indices calculated from bathymetry data to produce a potentially more robust method for delineating in these unique instances.

Using customized software, the texture procedure of Cutter et al. (2003) was modified by parameterizing the standard LFH feature vector. For the standard LFH, there are four component LFHs that comprise the complete LFH. Each of the component LFHs represents the distribution of value coefficients from discrete Fourier transforms applied to local grid cells. Instead of binning the local Fourier map (LFM) data to create a 32-element LFH feature vector, we calculated the feature vector elements that represent the mean and standard deviation of each component LFH. This process reduces the complete LFH from a 32-element feature vector to an 8-element feature vector (i.e. LFH0_mean, LFH0_StD, LFH1_mean, LFH1_StD, LFH2_mean, LFH2_StD, LFH3_mean, LFH3_StD) and provides a more concise description of the texture feature. Reducing data dimensionality was a necessity due to the computational requirements associated with populating a covariance matrix of more than 20 vectors for maximum likelihood classification (also the maximum allowable number of input raster bands when using Arcview Spatial Analyst MLClassify), and subsequently classifying each data point of a 1-meter grid across 90 km^2 of seafloor. After the parameterized LFH texture feature vectors were calculated on a per cell basis, the LFH1, LFH2, and LFH3 indices were reformatted into Arcview ascii grid format. To reduce classification impacts related to mean depth effects, LFH0 values were not used in the classification since it essentially represents the mean value of the data series.

Using video data from block 110_0204a, training classes were manually digitized in Arcview to define representative statistics for areas of four distinct backscatter signatures which corresponded to rock outcrop (h), mixed sediment of boulders, cobbles and sand (m(bcs)), soft sand (s(s)), and soft sand and shell with waves (s(sq)). This four class segmentation effectively corresponds to the bottom induration attribute described in Greene et al. (1999). To insure comparable results between blocks, the signature covariance matrix output from block 110_0204a was subsequently used to segment blocks 110_0204b and 110_0204c.

Using Arcview Spatial Analyst, a maximum likelihood classification procedure was then used to segment the data into the four distinct classes using the LFH indices (with exception of LFH0), backscatter intensity, and a simple standard deviation surface calculated from the bathymetry data as raster input layers (Figure 3). The resulting output raster was converted to a feature polygon layer and attributed according to Greene et al. (1999). Micro-scale habitat features were added to the polygons in areas where video groundtruthing was conducted.

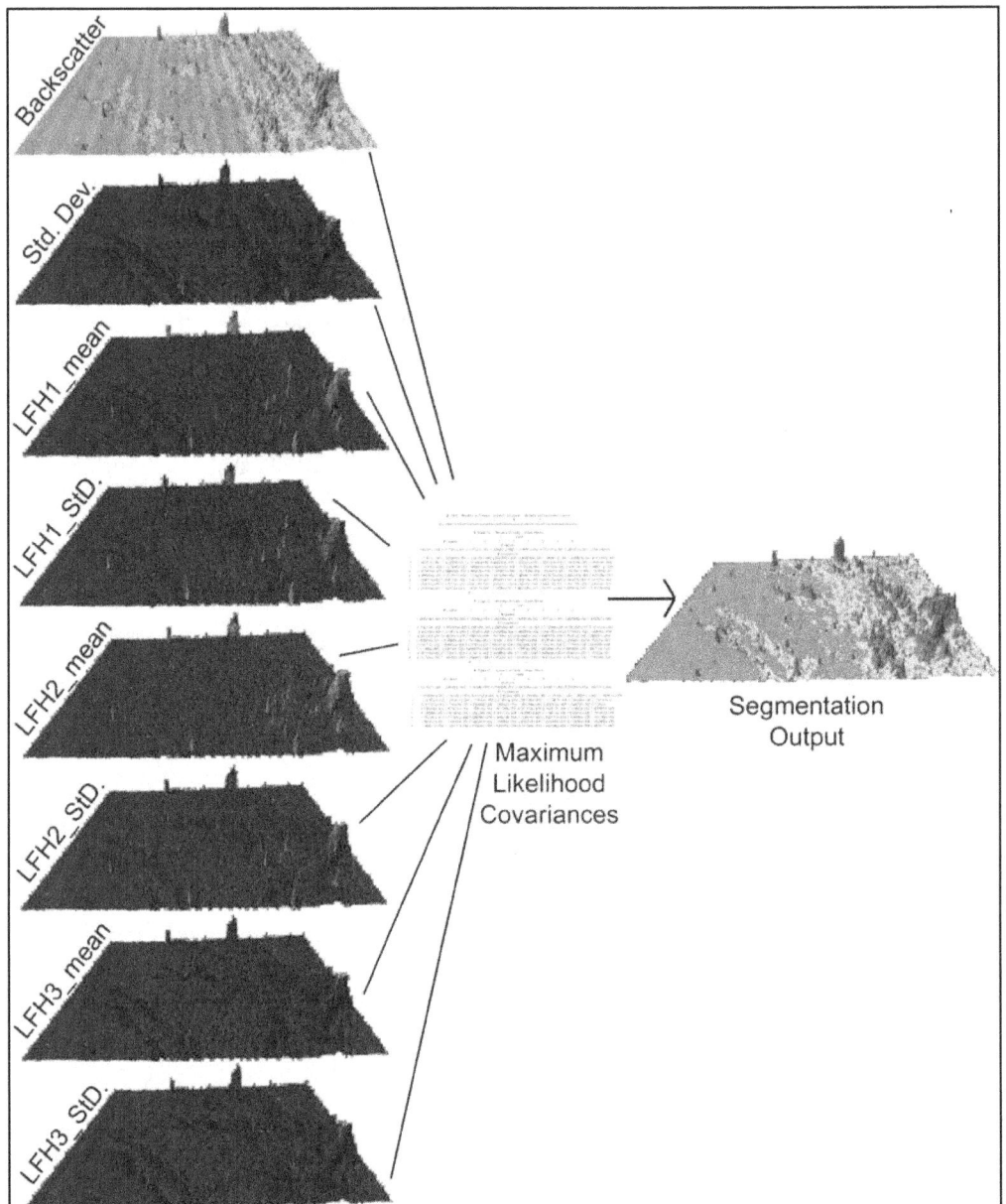

Figure 3. Schematic of data layers input into the Spatial Analyst maximum likelihood classification procedure. The eight layers represent backscatter intensity, standard deviation surface calculated from bathymetry data, and 6 LFH indices corresponding to the mean and standard deviation feature vectors of LFH1, LFH2, and LFH3. The LFH0 magnitude was not used in the classification since it basically represents the mean of the input data. Colors in the output grid correspond to rock outcrop (red), mixed substrate of boulders, cobble, and sand (yellow), and soft sand (blue). Scalar indices have been draped over bathymetry data to illustrate relief.

GROUNDTRUTHING

A camera sled was deployed from the NOAA research vessel *Tatoosh* on September 5 and 6, 2006 and September 4, 2007 to acquire underwater videography for assisting with sonar signature validation. The camera device was configured with a Deep Sea Power & Light SeaCam, SeaLite and dual SeaLasers, TriTech 200 kHz altimeter, and an Applied Acoustic micro beacon. Video was captured using a Sony GV-D1000 mini-DV recorder using a Sea-Trak GPS overlay to dub positioning information onto the video. Since no USBL positioning was available, the tow sled was drifted directly below the A-frame in an effort to minimize positional offset from the vessel's DGPS antennae. Due to scheduled vessel availability and unfavorable sea conditions, limited video effort was accomplished during each year.

Records extracted from the usSEABED project (Reid et al. 2006) provided 40 samples to further describe sedimentology within the survey area. Video transects and usSEABED sample locations are shown in Figure 4.

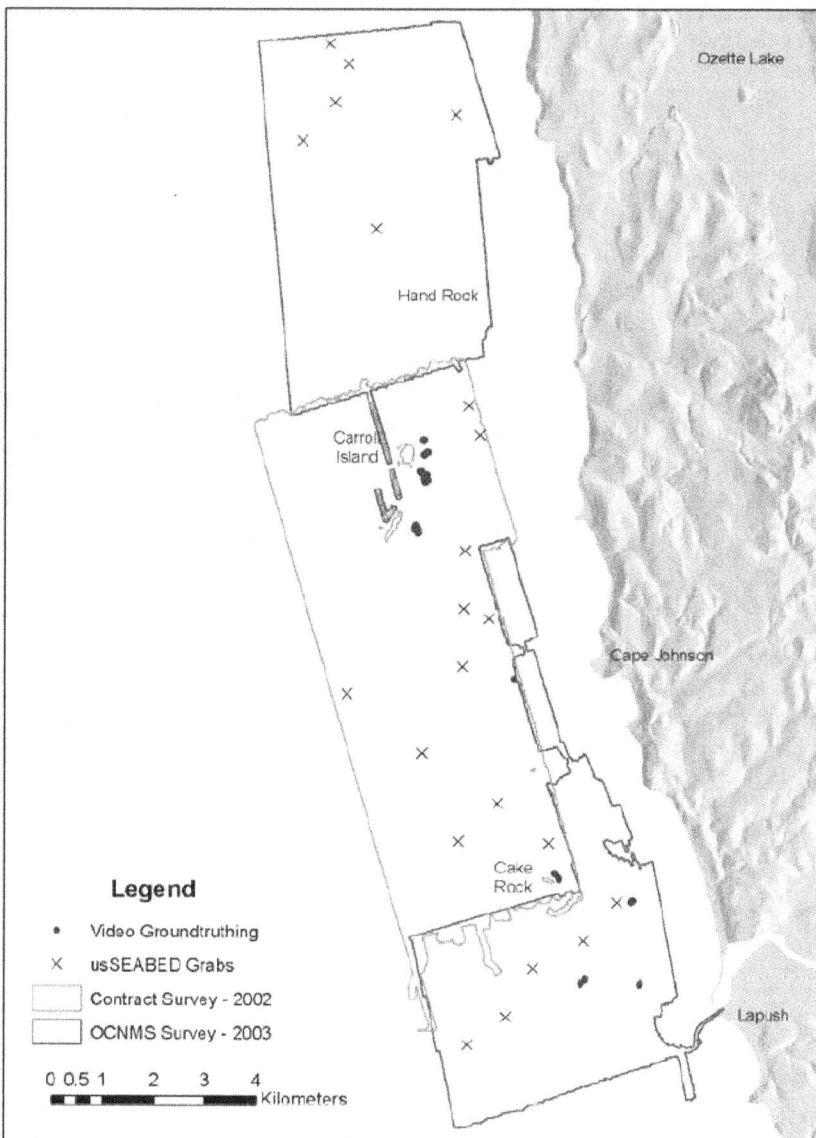

Figure 4. Location of groundtruthing validation in relation to individual survey blocks. Purple spheres define track lines of limited video confirmation, and black cross hairs indicate location of bottom samples extracted from the usSeabed database.

DISCUSSION OF SURVEY RESULTS AND INTERPRETATION

With effort of both vessels, over 1,300 linear km of MBES data were acquired and nearly 86 hours of actual logged sonar records were obtained throughout the area (Table 1).

Table 1. Below are the survey effort statistics for HMPR-110-2002-04. Reson 8101 MBES data were acquired aboard the *R/V MacGinitie* in 2002 (110_0204a) and *NOAA Ship Rainier* survey launch RA3 in 2003 (110_0204b and 110_0204c). Area is presented in square kilometers, length of linear track lines in kilometers, and hours of actual logged sonar packets in hours, minutes, and seconds.

Year	Survey Dates	Area (km^2)	Tracks (km)	Hours (h:m:s)
2002	July 27-Aug. 02	41.9	575.4	35:57:08
2003	Aug. 28-Sept. 25	49.0	754.4	49:55:28
Total		**90.9**	**1,329.8**	**85:52:36**

Substrate Segmentation

The LFH segmentation routine resulted in more than 75 percent of each block (Table 2, Figures 5-7) classified as unconsolidated sand and silt sediment, likely being of glacial origin (Dragovich et al. 2002). The remainder of each block was nearly split between hard, exposed rock outcrop and a mixed substrate consisting of boulder, cobble, gravel, and sand. Tabor and Cady (1978) suggest the cobble, gravel, and sands throughout this area are glacial deposits left over from the continental ice sheet. Several geologic maps (Tabor and Cady 1978; Rau 1979; Snavely et al. 1993; and Dragovich et al. 2002) additionally describe the majority of rock outcrops throughout the survey area as being marine sedimentary rocks of sandstone granular conglomerate, although the flanks of Cake Rock and many of the offshore rocks north toward Cape Johnson have been defined as basalt (Tabor and Cady 1978). James Island has additionally been described as massive to thick bedded greywacke sandstone (Rau 1979). However, for the purpose of this survey report all segmented rock outcrops were simply classified as hard, exposed rock outcrop according to Greene et al. (1999). Polygon segmentation results are presented in Figures 5-7, and shown with the adjacent survey block to illustrate classification continuity between blocks.

Table 2. Distribution of bottom hardness for each sonar block classified from survey HMPR-110-2002-04. See Figure 1 for area locations. Bottom hardness codes are hard (h), mixed (m) and soft (s) – additional class description classes provided above. Area is presented in square meters (top value) and percentage of each individual mapped area (bottom bold value in the matrix).

Year	Survey Block	h	m(bcs)	s(s)	s(sq)
2002	110_0204a	5,119,694	1,753,000	32,901,169	31,447
		12.86	**4.40**	**82.66**	**0.08**
2003	110_0204b	2,770,162	3,932,410	21,412,001	0
		9.85	**13.98**	**76.16**	**0.00**
2003	110_0204c	2,479,180	2,184,399	17,524,119	0
		11.17	**9.85**	**78.98**	**0.00**

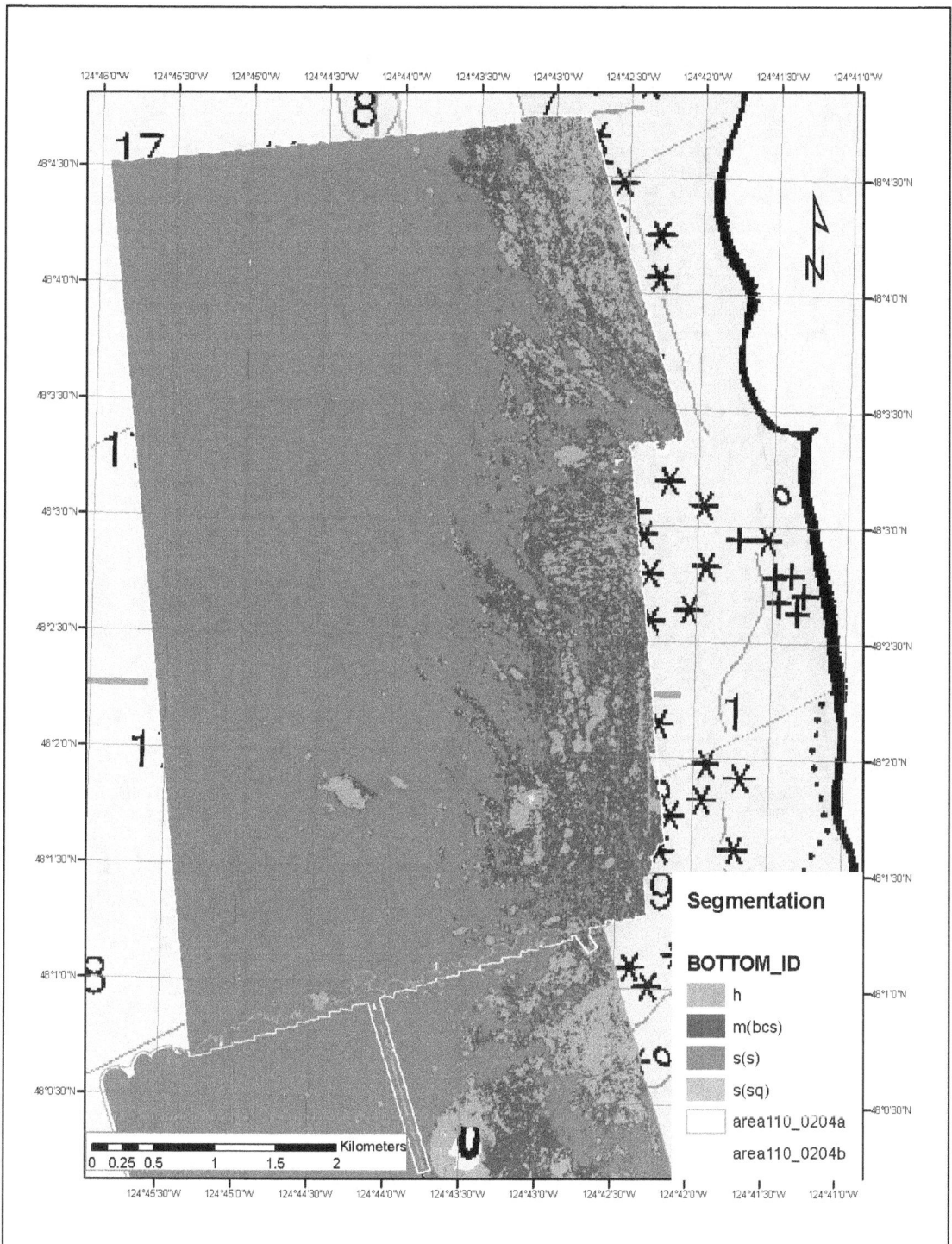

Figure 5. Seafloor substrate polygons, Ozette Lake to Carroll Island, with bottom_id codes taken from Greene et al. (1999). Classing generated through maximum likelihood LFH segmentation with further refinement from video observation. h=hard bottom; m(bcs)=mixed sediment of boulders, cobble and sand; s(s)=soft sandy bottom; s(sq)=soft sandy bottom with shell hash.

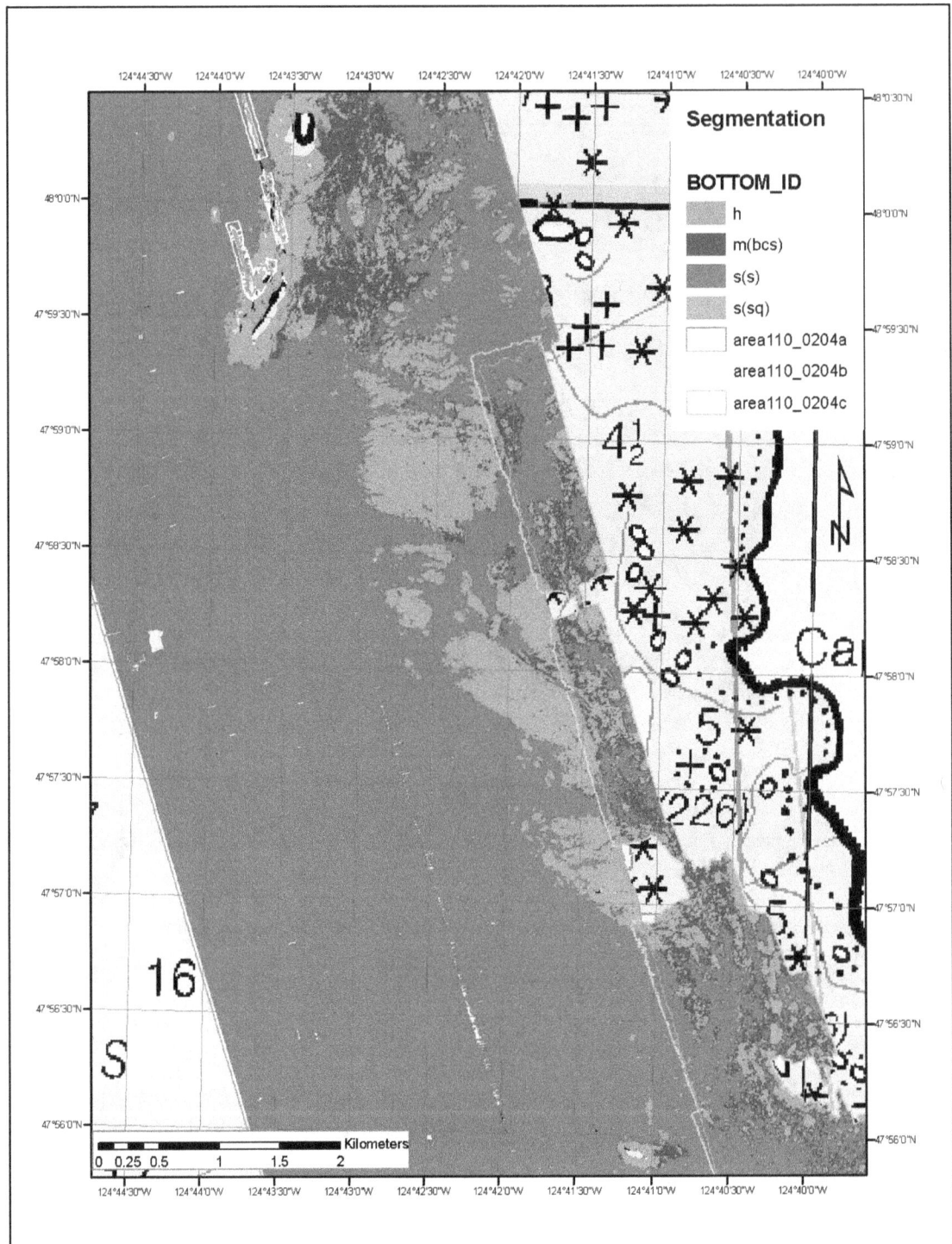

Figure 6. Seafloor substrate polygons, Carroll Island to Cake Rock, with bottom_id codes taken from Greene et al. (1999). Classing generated through maximum likelihood LFH segmentation with further refinement from video observation. h=hard bottom; m(bcs)=mixed sediment of boulders, cobble and sand; s(s)=soft sandy bottom; s(sq)=soft sandy bottom with shell hash.

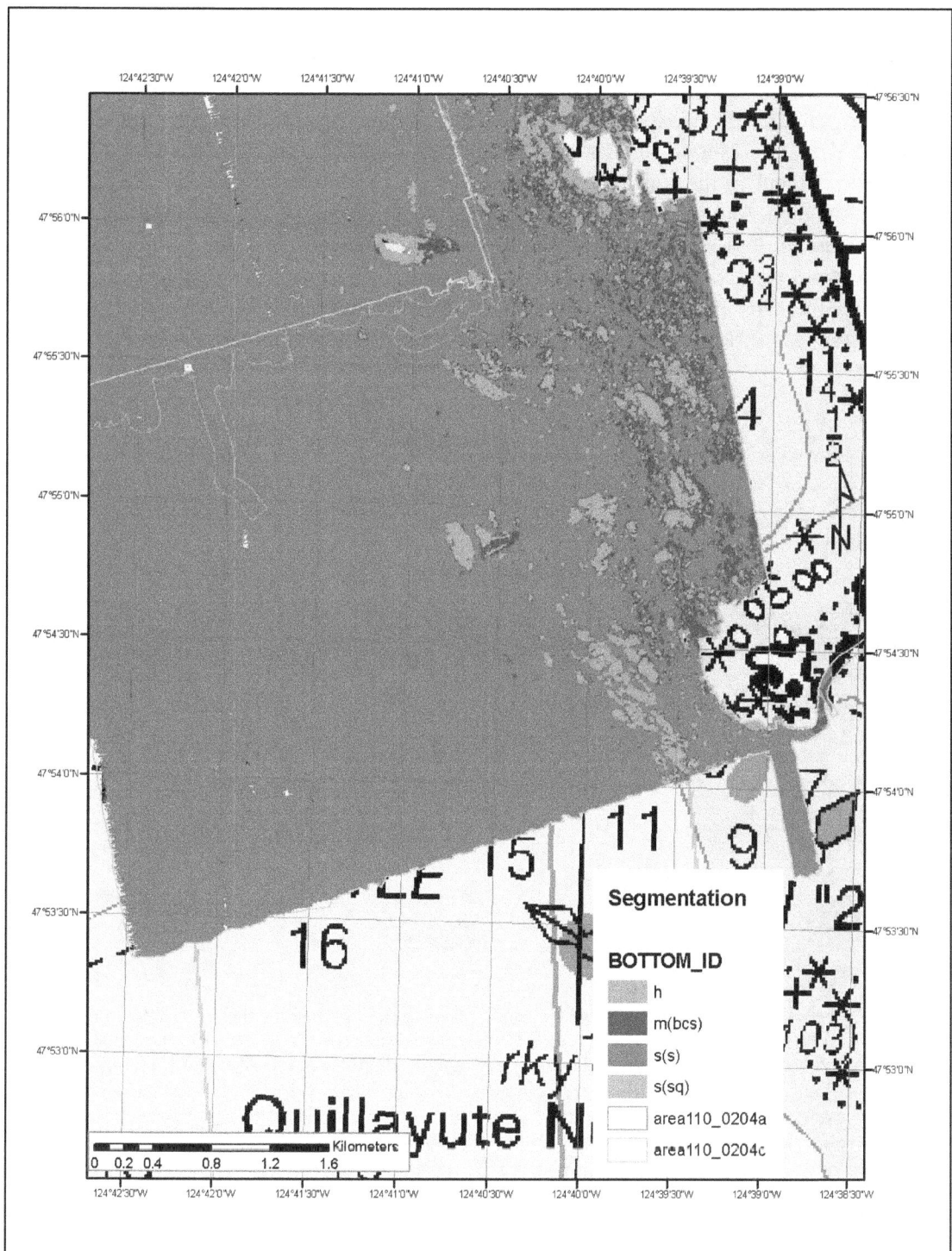

Figure 7. Seafloor substrate polygons, Cake Rock to James Island, with bottom_id codes taken from Greene et al. (1999). Classing generated through maximum likelihood LFH segmentation with further refinement from video observation. h=hard bottom; m(bcs)=mixed sediment of boulders, cobble and sand; s(s)=soft sandy bottom; s(sq)=soft sandy bottom with shell hash.

A processed bathymetry surface and backscatter mosaics are additionally presented in Appendices 2 and 3, respectively. By modifying the LFH method introduced by Cutter et al. (2003) and additionally incorporating backscatter intensity, we were successful at segmenting adjacent areas with homogenous roughness into unique classes. For example, Figure 8 shows a flat region of the seafloor with minimal deviation in roughness, evident in the standard deviation surface shown at left. Within this same flat homogenous area, a unique backscatter signature (delineated by the red outline) exists in the plate shown at right. Video groundtruthing further revealed this particular area to consist of sand waves mixed with shell hash transitioning into a soft sand field. Adding backscatter intensity as a textural descriptor into the maximum likelihood rule increased our effectiveness at delineating these particular substrate types in other areas.

Figure 8. Example of homogenous bathymetry and unique backscatter signature as segmented by the modified LFH procedure. Standard deviation bathymetry surface at left and backscatter intensity at right. Video groundtruthing (light green track) revealed area defined in red as sand and shell hash with waves, transitioning into a soft sand field (blue track line). Large boulders (purple) and rock outcrop (pink) were also observed in video collected nearby.

Although minimal groundtruthing was captured due to vessel availability further constrained by weather conditions, the limited video data indicated the modified LFH procedure could successfully segment the imagery into four classes that broadly represent distinct substrate conditions. It should be noted, however, that ground conditions may have changed during the 4 year period that span the acoustic and video surveys. It is entirely conceivable, for example, that previously exposed outcrops may have become reburied in sand, and vice versa, thus potentially complicating validation.

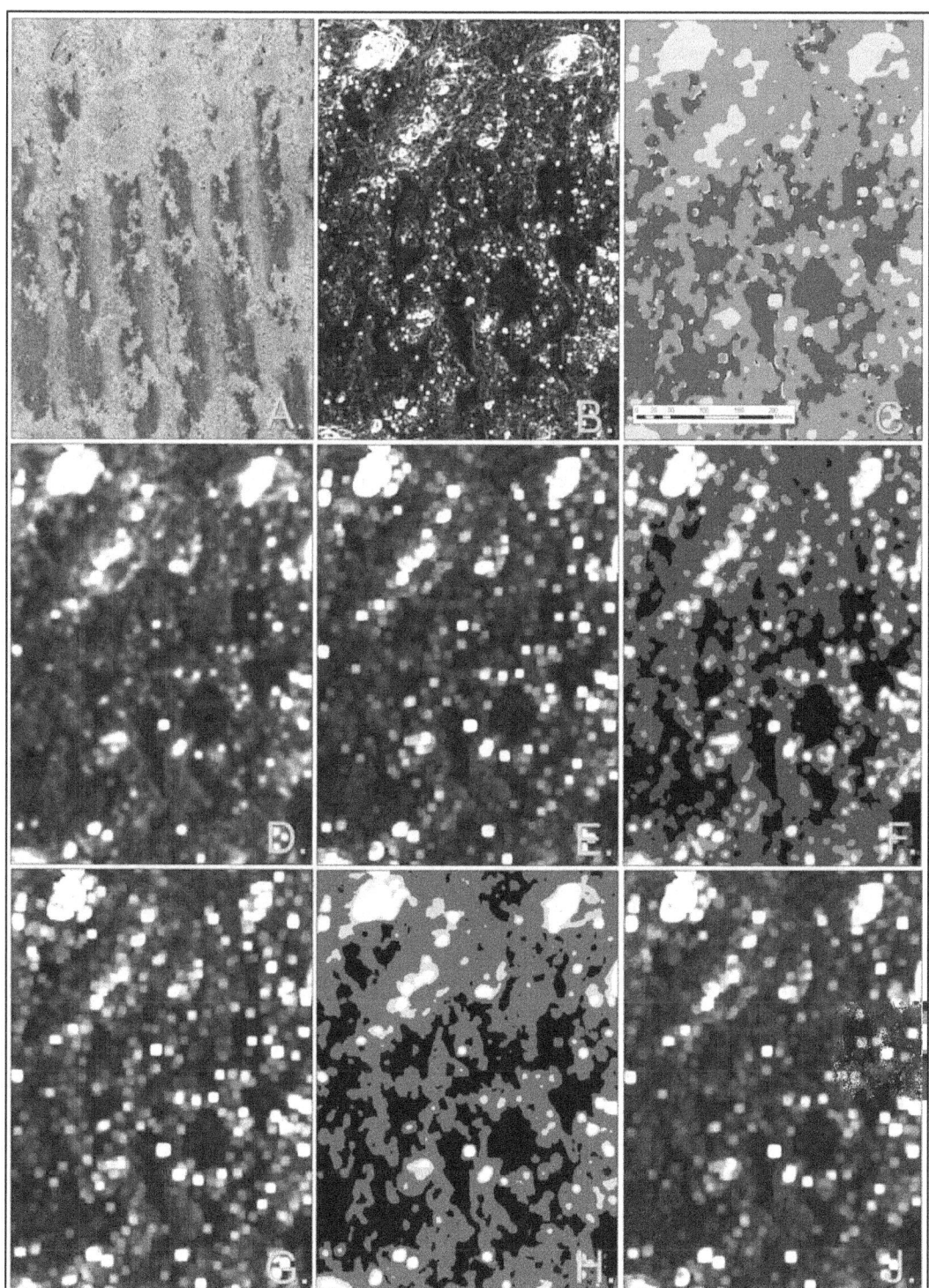

Figure 9. Example of data layers to the maximum likelihood classification routine (except C) with resulting segmentation output (C). Individual extractions shown include backscatter mosaic (A); standard deviation surface (3x3 window) calculated from multibeam bathymetry (B); LFH1_mean (D); LFH1_StD. (E); LFH2_mean (F); LFH2_StD. (G); LFH3_mean (H); LFH3_StD. (J). Segmentation results in plate C correspond to soft sand (blue), mixed sediment of boulder, cobble and sand (red), and exposed rock outcrop (yellow).

13

By creating mean and standard deviation feature vectors for each of the 4 feature magnitudes, the LFH dimensionality was reduced from a 32-element vector to an 8-element vector while maintaining the ability to successfully segment the data and without crippling computers during computation. The textural variation maintained by the mean and standard deviation LFH magnitudes can be seen in Figure 9.

The technique avoided the subjective manual editing that OCNMS has experienced in the past when using grey-scale covariance indices as a classification method. The LFH texture indices further provided an objective means for incorporating bathymetry characteristics without having to subjectively define classes based on slope or complexity criteria. Exchanging the standard deviation bathymetry input layer with one calculated from a rugosity index may provide even more robust results, especially along flat and sloping interfaces. Future work will focus on the effectiveness of calculating LFH indices from side scan sonar data alone, and investigate the ability of the technique to segment imagery without associated bathymetry data.

The ability to remotely define EFH could benefit from output produced by this efficient, reproducible, and robust means of segmenting MBES data by defining numerous seafloor substrate characteristics important to federally managed species of concern. Although geomorphic properties of the seafloor can now be remotely characterized with some degree of relative efficiency (Figure 10) they provide only a piece of the EFH puzzle. To more adequately describe EFH, additional sampling protocol is needed to gain a better understanding of the many other physical and environmental processes (besides seafloor substrate) that are important to the biota (McConnaughey et al. 2007). Having data sources to populate a multitude of variables may provide better proxies for ultimately modeling distribution of commercially important species.

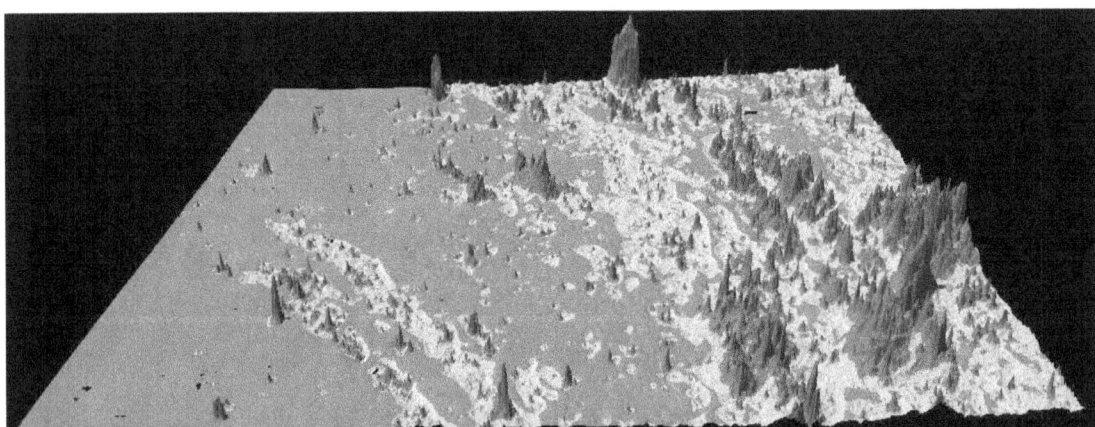

Figure 10. Clipped section of area1 10_0204b, illustrating a geomorphic representation of seafloor substrates produced through the LFH texture segmentation of acoustic MBES data. Scalar Bottom_Id values from Greene et al. (1999) are draped over the associated bathymetry data showing areas of soft sand (light blue), mixed substrate of boulders, cobbles, and sand (yellow), and rock outcrop (red).

14

Bathymetry Data

Previous knowledge of seafloor in this area was not well documented. In fact, the nautical chart covering the survey area (18480) is one the of the smallest scale charts (1:176,000) released along the west coast with previously charted soundings throughout this particular survey area being estimated from partial bottom coverage surveys obtained between 1900-1939. These full bottom coverage surveys conducted in 2002 and 2003 identified numerous uncharted features and/or potential chart misrepresentations and will be forwarded to NOAAs Office of Coast Survey for further scrutiny. A few interesting rock features identified are presented in Figure 11.

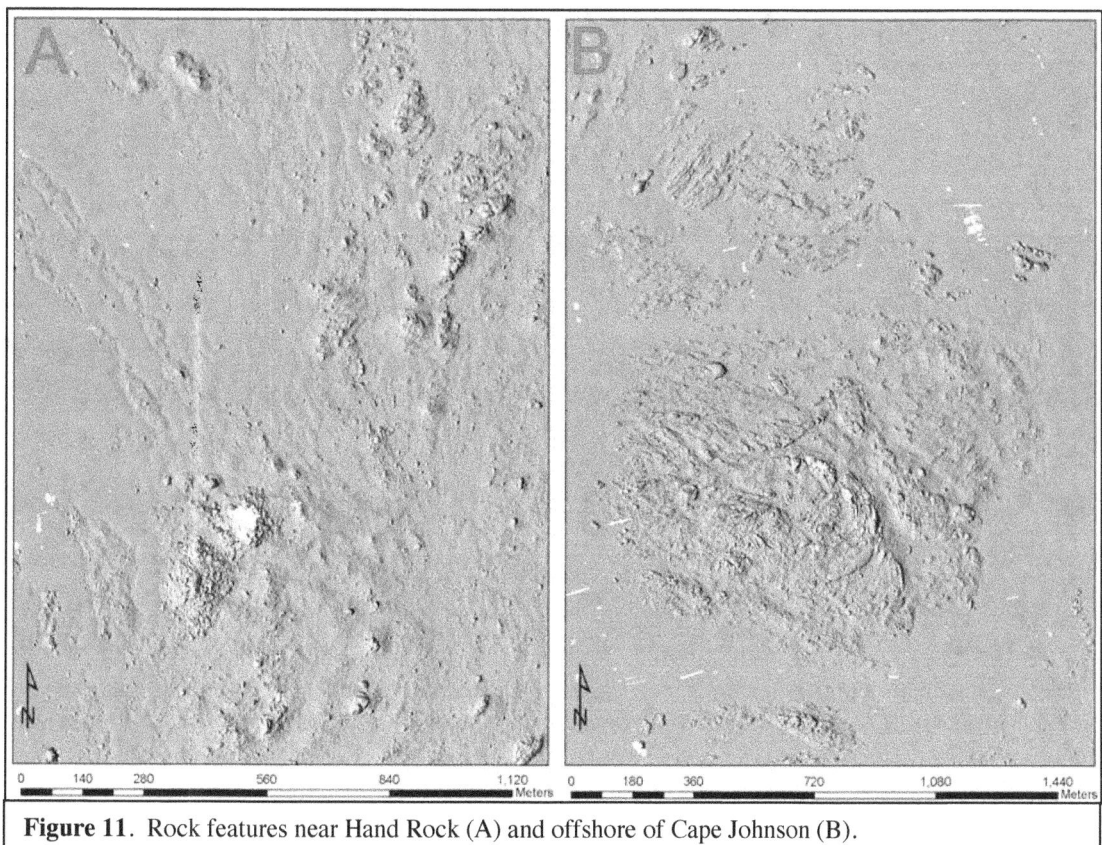

Figure 11. Rock features near Hand Rock (A) and offshore of Cape Johnson (B).

The bathymetry data collected in 2002 (block 110_0204a) suffered from sound velocity refraction problems (Figure 12) especially evident in the most western lines where water depths were greatest and sediments consisted of the soft alluvial sand characteristic of lower backscatter strength. As accurate depth estimates depend greatly on reduced sound speed errors, significant time was spent attempting post-processing "correction" of the 2002 data using the Caris refraction editor. There were no refraction artifacts in the 2003 survey, likely because sound speed profiles were more frequently measured each survey day. On average, sound speed profiles were collected for each 3.7 hours of data acquisition during the 2002 survey and for each 1.7 hours of surveying in 2003 (Table 3).

Since the Reson 8101 MBES is not a flat-head transducer, its barrel-like physical shape determines initial transmit geometry during each ping cycle. This particular type of transducer, therefore, assumes the correct sound departure angle already exists at time of transmit and any subsequent error in sound velocity measurements will translate into additional errors in the estimated depth values (Cartwright and Hughes Clarke 2002). As fresh water input from the Quileute River near Lapush can impact salinity in this area, and thus sound refraction, it is evident that more frequent sound velocity casts become critical to minimizing refraction artifacts in these types of areas.

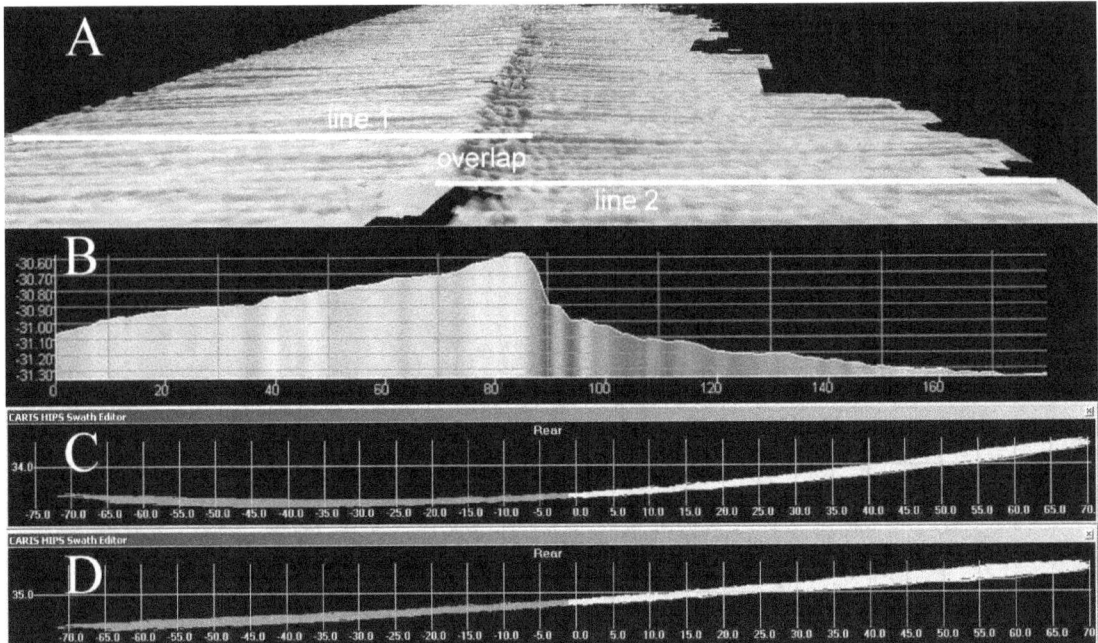

Figure 12. Example of refraction artifact encountered in the 2002 survey data with overlap of adjacent lines shown in inset A, and a depth cross-section of these same two lines illustrated in inset B. The result of refraction in this area is evident by the approximate half meter "false rise" in the middle of the insets where the two outer edges of each line overlap. Additional refraction is illustrated in unedited data (C) as the apparent "upward bending" of the outer swath edges. Inset D shows the result of post-processing refraction editing of this same swath.

16

Table 3. Frequency of sound velocity (sv) casts acquired each day during the 2002 and 2003 surveys. Hours surveyed (h:m:s) refers to the amount of logged MBES data collected in a given day.

Survey Group	Survey Year	Julian Day	# of Daily SV Casts	Hours Surveyed	Hours Surveying Per Cast
CSUMB	2002	209	1	2:03:35	2.1
		210	2	5:29:27	2.7
		211	2	5:21:41	2.7
		212	2	7:01:52	3.5
		213	2	7:33:28	3.8
		214	2	8:27:05	4.2
OCNMS	2003	237	1	0:59:38	1.0
		240	2	5:32:43	2.8
		241	3	6:32:21	2.2
		248	4	3:44:25	0.9
		251	3	5:11:54	1.7
		258	5	5:31:46	1.1
		259	3	3:54:35	1.3
		260	3	3:42:56	1.2
		265	2	3:37:42	1.8
		266	2	5:01:56	2.5
		267	2	4:37:57	2.3

ACKNOWLEDGMENTS

The authors would like to thank the *NOAA Ship Rainier* for access to the survey launch in 2003, and David Kirner, Andy Palmer and Wally Pierce for safely skippering the vessel in a challenging near shore environment. Additional thanks to David Kirner and Mike Levine for skippering the *R/V Tatoosh* during groundtruthing efforts.

REFERENCES

Alee, R.J. M. Dethier, D. Brown, L.F. Deegan, R.G. Ford, T.F. Hourigan, J. Maragos, C. Schoch, K. Sealey, R. Twilley, M.P. Weinstein, and M. Yaklovich, 2000, U.S. Marine and estuarine ecosystem and habitat classification system. NOAA Tech. Memo. NMFS-F/SPO-43.

Beaudoin, J., Hughes Clarke, J.E., Van den Ameele, E. and Gardner, J., 2002, Geometric and radiometric correction of multibeam backscatter derived from Reson 8101 systems: Canadian Hydrographic Conference 2002 Proceedings (CDROM), Toronto, Canada.

Calder, B.R. and L.A. Mayer. 2003. Automatic processing of high-rate, high-density multibeam echosounder data. Geochem. 4(6):1048-1064.

Carlson, H.R. and R.R. Straty. 1981. Habitat and nursery grounds of Pacific rockfish, *Sebastes* spp., in rocky coastal areas of Southeastern Alaska. Marine Fisheries Review 43:13-19.

Cartwright, D.S. and J.E. Hughes Clarke. 2002. Multibeam surveys on the Fraser River Delta, coping with an extreme refraction environment. 2002 Canadian Hydrographic Conference Proceedings.

Cochrane, G.R., and K.D. Lafferty. 2002. Use of acoustic classification of sidescan sonar data for mapping benthic habitat in the Northern Channel Islands, California. Continental Shelf Research 22: 683-690.

Cutter, G.R. Jr., Y. Rzhanov, L.A. Mayer. 2003. Automated segmentation of seafloor bathymetry from multibeam echosounder data using local Fourier histogram texture features. Journal of Experimental Marine Biology and Ecology. 285-286: 355-370.

Dartnell, P. and J. Gardner. 2004. Predicting seafloor facies from multibeam bathymetry and backscatter data. Photogrammetric Engineering and Remote Sensing. 70(9): 1081-1091.

Dragovich J.D., R.L. Logan, H.W Schasse, T.J. Walsh, W.S. Lingley Jr., D.K. Norman, W.J. Gerstel, T.J. Lapen, J.E. Schuster, and K.D. Meyers. 2002. Geologic map of Washington-Northwest Quadrant. Washington Division of Geology and Earth Resources. Geologic Map GM-50.

Greene, H.G., M.M. Yoklavich, R.M. Starr, V.M. O'Connell, W.W. Wakefield, D.E. Sullivan, J.E. McRea, Jr., G.M. Cailliet. 1999. A classification scheme for deep seafloor habitats. Oceanologica Acta. 22(6):663

Harney, J. N., G.R. Cochrane, L.L. Etherington, P. Dartnell, N.E. Golden, and H. Chezar. 2006. Geologic characteristics of benthic habitats in Glacier Bay, Southeast Alaska. Version 1.0. U.S. Geological Survey. Open-File Report 2006-1081.

Intelmann, S.S. and G.R. Cochrane. 2006a. Benthic Habitat Mapping in the Olympic Coast National Marine Sanctuary: Classification of side scan sonar data from survey HMPR- 108-2002-01: Version I. Marine Sanctuaries Conservation Series MSD-06-01. U.S. Department of Commerce, National Oceanic and Atmospheric Administration, Marine Sanctuaries Division, Silver Spring, MD. 22pp.

Intelmann, S.S. and G.R. Cochrane. 2006b. Olympic Coast National Marine Sanctuary Habitat Mapping: Survey report and classification of side scan sonar data from surveys HMPR-114-2004-02 and HMPR-116-2005-01. Marine Sanctuaries Conservation Series MSD-06-07. U.S. Department of Commerce, National Oceanic and Atmospheric Administration, National Marine Sanctuary Program, Silver Spring, MD. 35 pp.

Intelmann, S.S., J. Beaudoin, and G.R. Cochrane. 2006. Normalization and characterization of multibeam backscatter: Koitlah Point to Point of the Arches, Olympic Coast National Marine Sanctuary - Survey HMPR-115-2004-03. Marine Sanctuaries Conservation Series MSD-06-03. U.S. Department of Commerce, National Oceanic and Atmospheric Administration, Marine Sanctuaries Division, Silver Spring, MD. 22pp.

Intelmann, S.S., G.R. Cochrane, C. E. Bowlby, M.S. Brancato, and J. Hyland. 2007. Survey report of NOAA Ship McArthur II cruises AR-04-04, AR-05-05 and AR-06-03: Habitat classification of side scan sonar imagery in support of deep-sea coral/sponge explorations at the Olympic Coast National Marine Sanctuary. Marine Sanctuaries Conservation Series MSD-07-01. U.S. Department of Commerce, National Oceanic and Atmospheric Administration, National Marine Sanctuary Program, Silver Spring, MD. 50 pp.

Kostylev, V.E., B.J. Todd, G.B. Fader, R.C. Courtney, G.D. Cameron, and R.A. Pickerill. 2001. Benthic habitat mapping on the Scotian Shelf based on multibeam bathymetry, surficial geology and sea floor photographs. Marine Ecology. Progress Series 219:121-137.

Krieger, K.J. 1993. Distribution and abundance of rockfish determined from a submersible and by bottom trawling. Fishery Bulletin 91:87-96.

Love, M.S., M.H. Carr, and L.J. Haldorson. 1991. The ecology of substrate associated juveniles of the genus *Sebastes*. Environmental Biology of Fishes 30:225-243.

Magnuson-Stevens Act Provisions: Essential Fish Habitat (EFH), Final Rule." Federal Register 67, Fed. Reg: 2343-2383 (Jan. 17, 2002) (to be codified at 50 CFR pt. 600.

Mayer, L.A., J. Hughes-Clarke, and S. Dijkstra. 1999. Multibeam sonar: potential applications for fisheries research. Journal of Shellfish Research. 17: 1463-1467.

McConnaughey, R., and K. Smith. 2000. Associations between flatfish abundance and surficial sediments in the eastern Bering Sea. Canadian Journal of Fisheries and Aquatic Sciences. 57(12):2410-2419.

McConnaughey, B., C. Yeung, S. Syrjala, K. Smith. 2007. Mapping environmental variables to model essential fish habitat. Conference Poster: Marine Habitat Mapping Technology Workshop for Alaska, Anchorage, AK, Apr 2007.

Rau, W.W. 1979. Geologic map in the vicinity of the lower Bogachiel and Hoh River Valleys, and the Washington Coast. Geologic Map GM 24. State of Washington Department of Natural Resources

Reid, J.A., J.M. Reid, C.J. Jenkins, M. Zimmermann, S.J. Williams, and M.E. Field. 2006. usSEABED: Pacific Coast (California, Oregon, Washington) offshore surficial-sediment data release: U.S. Geological Survey Data Series 182, version 1.0. Online at http://pubs.usgs.gov/ds/2006/182/

Reson 2003. SeaBat 8101 Multibeam echosounder system operator's manual. Version 3.01.

Snavely, P.D., Jr., N.S. MacLeod, and A.R. Niem. 1993. Geologic Map of the Cape Flattery, Clallam Bay, Ozette Lake, and Lake Pleasant Quadrangles, Northwestern Olympic Peninsula, Washington. Map I-1946. U.S. Geological Survey.

Stein, D.L., B. N. Tissot, M.A. Hixon, and W. Barss, 1992. Fish-habitat associations on a deep reef at the edge of the Oregon continental shelf, Fishery Bulletin, 90:540-551.

Tabor, R.W., and W.M. Cady. 1978. Geologic map of the Olympic Peninsula, Washington. Map I-994. U.S. Geological Survey.

Todd, B.J., G.B.J. Fader, R.C. Courtney, R.A. Pickrill. 1999. Quaternary geology and surficial sediment processes; Browns Bank, Scotian Shelf; based on multibeam bathymetry. Marine Geology 162(1), 165-214.

APPENDIX

Appendix 1. Vessel Offsets

R/V MacGinitie

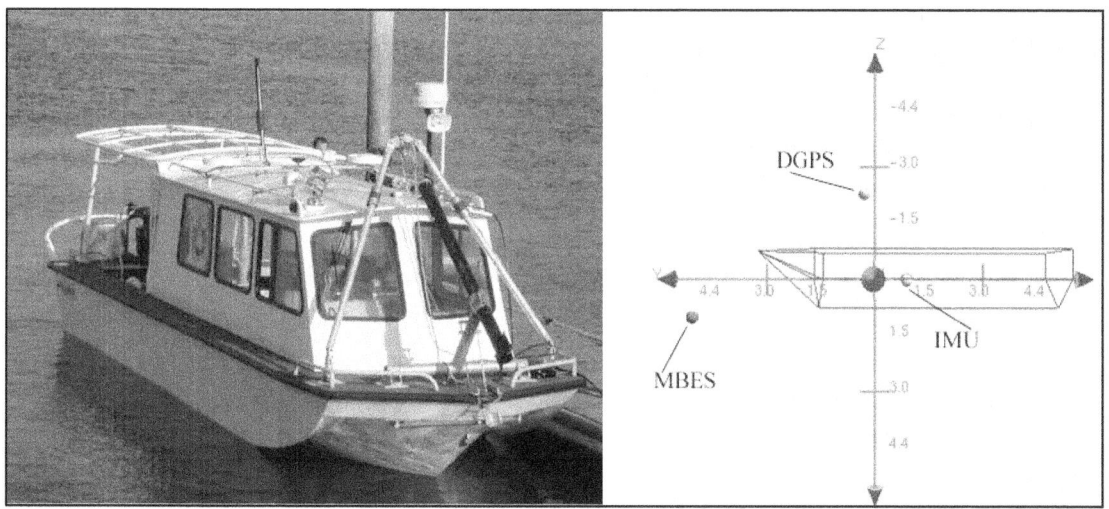

```xml
<?xml version="1.0"?>
<HIPSVesselConfig Version="2.0">
 <VesselShape>
  <PlanCoordinates>
   <Entry X="-1.300000" Y="-4.100000"/>
   <Entry X="1.300000" Y="-4.100000"/>
   <Entry X="1.300000" Y="2.400000"/>
   <Entry X="0.000000" Y="4.100000"/>
   <Entry X="-1.300000" Y="2.400000"/>
   <Entry X="-1.300000" Y="-4.100000"/>
  </PlanCoordinates>
  <ProfileCoordinates>
   <Entry Y="-4.100000" Z="0.750000"/>
   <Entry Y="-4.100000" Z="-0.750000"/>
   <Entry Y="2.400000" Z="-0.750000"/>
   <Entry Y="4.100000" Z="0.750000"/>
   <Entry Y="-4.100000" Z="0.750000"/>
  </ProfileCoordinates>
  <RP Length="4.100000" Width="1.300000" Height="0.750000"/>
 </VesselShape>
 <DepthSensor>
  <TimeStamp value="2002-200 00:00:00">
   <Latency value="0.000000"/>
   <SensorClass value="Swath"/>
   <TransducerEntries>
    <Transducer Number="1" Model="sb8101">
```

```
    <Offsets X="0.000000" Y="5.890000" Z="1.000000" Latency="0.000000"/>
    <MountAngle Pitch="-6.700000" Roll="0.800000" Azimuth="1.500000"/>
   </Transducer>
   </TransducerEntries>
  </TimeStamp>
</DepthSensor>
<DraftSensor>
 <TimeStamp value="2002-200 00:00:00">
  <Comment value="(null)"/>
  <Latency value="0.000000"/>
  <ApplyFlag value="No"/>
  <DraftEntries/>
 </TimeStamp>
</DraftSensor>
<GyroSensor>
 <TimeStamp value="2002-200 00:00:00">
  <Latency value="0.000000"/>
  <ApplyFlag value="No"/>
 </TimeStamp>
</GyroSensor>
<HeaveSensor>
 <TimeStamp value="2002-200 00:00:00">
  <Comment value="(null)"/>
  <Latency value="0.000000"/>
  <Manufacturer value="(null)"/>
  <Model value="(null)"/>
  <SerialNumber value="(null)"/>
  <ApplyFlag value="Yes"/>
  <Offsets X="-0.060000" Y="0.000000" Z="0.030000"/>
 </TimeStamp>
</HeaveSensor>
<NavSensor>
 <TimeStamp value="2002-200 00:00:00">
  <Comment value="(null)"/>
  <Latency value="0.050000"/>
  <Manufacturer value="(null)"/>
  <Model value="(null)"/>
  <SerialNumber value="(null)"/>
  <Ellipse value="WG84"/>
  <Offsets X="-0.040000" Y="1.180000" Z="-2.240000"/>
 </TimeStamp>
</NavSensor>
<PitchSensor>
 <TimeStamp value="2002-200 00:00:00">
  <Latency value="0.000000"/>
  <ApplyFlag value="Yes"/>
```

        <Offsets Pitch="0.000000"/>
      </TimeStamp>
    </PitchSensor>
    <RollSensor>
      <TimeStamp value="2002-200 00:00:00">
        <Latency value="0.000000"/>
        <ApplyFlag value="Yes"/>
        <Offsets Roll="0.000000"/>
      </TimeStamp>
    </RollSensor>
    <SVPSensor>
      <TimeStamp value="2002-200 00:00:00">
        <Latency value="0.000000"/>
        <DualHead value="Yes"/>
        <Offsets X="0.000000" Y="5.890000" Z="1.000000" X2="0.000000"
Y2="0.000000" Z2="0.000000"/>
        <MountAngle Pitch="0.000000" Roll="0.000000" Azimuth="0.000000"
Pitch2="0.000000" Roll2="0.000000" Azimuth2="0.000000"/>
      </TimeStamp>
    </SVPSensor>
    <TPEConfiguration>
      <TimeStamp value="2002-200 00:00:00">
        <Comment value="ss intelmann"/>
        <Latency value="0.000000"/>
        <Offsets>
          <MRUtoTransducer X="0.060000" Y="5.890000" Z="0.070000" X2="0.000000"
Y2="0.000000" Z2="0.000000"/>
          <NavigationToTransducer X="-0.040000" Y="4.710000" Z="3.240000"
X2="0.000000" Y2="0.000000" Z2="0.000000"/>
          <Transducer Roll="0.000000" Roll2="0.000000"/>
          <Navigation Latency="0.000000"/>
        </Offsets>
        <StandardDeviation>
          <Motion Gyro="0.020000" HeavePercAmplitude="5.000000" Heave="0.050000"
Roll="0.050000" Pitch="0.050000" PitchStablized="0.000000"/>
          <Position Navigation="0.700000"/>
          <Timing Transducer="0.010000" Navigation="0.010000" Gyro-"0.010000"
Heave="0.010000" Pitch="0.010000" Roll="0.010000"/>
          <SoundVelocity Measured="0.500000" Surface="0.500000"/>
          <Tide Measured="0.010000" Zoning="0.200000"/>
          <Offsets X="0.020000" Y="0.020000" Z="0.020000"/>
          <MRUAlignment Gyro="0.000000" Pitch="0.000000" Roll="0.000000"/>
          <Vessel Speed="0.030000" Loading="0.050000" Draft="0.100000"
DeltaDraft="0.010000"/>
        </StandardDeviation>
      </TimeStamp>

```
  </TPEConfiguration>
  <WaterlineHeight>
   <TimeStamp value="2002-200 00:00:00">
    <Latency value="0.000000"/>
    <WaterLine value="0.000000"/>
    <ApplyFlag value="Yes"/>
    <StdDev Waterline="0.000000"/>
   </TimeStamp>
  </WaterlineHeight>
</HIPSVesselConfig>
```

NOAAS Rainier RA3 Survey Launch

```
<?xml version="1.0"?>
<HIPSVesselConfig Version="2.0">
  <VesselShape>
   <PlanCoordinates>
    <Entry X="-1.500000" Y="-4.500000"/>
    <Entry X="1.500000" Y="-4.500000"/>
    <Entry X="1.500000" Y="1.500000"/>
    <Entry X="0.000000" Y="4.500000"/>
    <Entry X="-1.500000" Y="1.500000"/>
    <Entry X="-1.500000" Y="-4.500000"/>
   </PlanCoordinates>
   <ProfileCoordinates>
    <Entry Y="-4.500000" Z="1.000000"/>
    <Entry Y="-4.500000" Z="-1.000000"/>
    <Entry Y="1.500000" Z="-1.000000"/>
    <Entry Y="4.500000" Z="1.000000"/>
```

```
      <Entry Y="-4.500000" Z="1.000000"/>
    </ProfileCoordinates>
    <RP Length="4.500000" Width="1.500000" Height="1.000000"/>
  </VesselShape>
  <DepthSensor>
   <TimeStamp value="2003-223 00:00:00">
    <Latency value="0.000000"/>
    <SensorClass value="Swath"/>
    <TransducerEntries>
     <Transducer Number="1" StartBeam="1" Model="sb8101">
      <Offsets X="0.330000" Y="0.330000" Z="0.680000" Latency="0.000000"/>
      <MountAngle Pitch="1.450000" Roll="0.170000" Azimuth="0.000000"/>
     </Transducer>
    </TransducerEntries>
   </TimeStamp>
  </DepthSensor>
  <DraftSensor>
   <TimeStamp value="2003-223 00:00:00">
    <Comment value="(null)"/>
    <Latency value="0.000000"/>
    <ApplyFlag value="Yes"/>
    <DraftEntries>
     <Entry Speed="0.000000" Draft="0.000000"/>
     <Entry Speed="7.775378" Draft="-0.010000"/>
     <Entry Speed="10.107991" Draft="0.010000"/>
     <Entry Speed="11.468683" Draft="0.010000"/>
     <Entry Speed="12.829374" Draft="0.020000"/>
     <Entry Speed="14.190065" Draft="0.030000"/>
     <Entry Speed="15.356372" Draft="0.030000"/>
     <Entry Speed="15.939525" Draft="0.030000"/>
     <Entry Speed="18.466523" Draft="0.000000"/>
    </DraftEntries>
   </TimeStamp>
  </DraftSensor>
  <GyroSensor>
   <TimeStamp value="2003-223 00:00:00">
    <Latency value="0.000000"/>
    <ApplyFlag value="No"/>
   </TimeStamp>
  </GyroSensor>
  <HeaveSensor>
   <TimeStamp value="2003-223 00:00:00">
    <Comment value="(null)"/>
    <Latency value="0.000000"/>
    <Manufacturer value="(null)"/>
    <Model value="(null)"/>
```

```xml
      <SerialNumber value="(null)"/>
      <ApplyFlag value="Yes"/>
      <Offsets X="0.000000" Y="0.480000" Z="0.160000"/>
     </TimeStamp>
   </HeaveSensor>
   <NavSensor>
     <TimeStamp value="2003-223 00:00:00">
      <Comment value="(null)"/>
      <Latency value="-0.200000"/>
      <Manufacturer value="(null)"/>
      <Model value="(null)"/>
      <SerialNumber value="(null)"/>
      <Ellipse value="WG84"/>
      <Offsets X="0.000000" Y="0.480000" Z="0.160000"/>
     </TimeStamp>
   </NavSensor>
   <PitchSensor>
     <TimeStamp value="2003-223 00:00:00">
      <Latency value="0.000000"/>
      <ApplyFlag value="Yes"/>
      <Offsets Pitch="0.000000"/>
     </TimeStamp>
   </PitchSensor>
   <RollSensor>
     <TimeStamp value="2003-223 00:00:00">
      <Latency value="0.000000"/>
      <ApplyFlag value="Yes"/>
      <Offsets Roll="0.000000"/>
     </TimeStamp>
   </RollSensor>
   <SVPSensor>
     <TimeStamp value="2003-223 00:00:00">
      <Comment value="(null)"/>
      <Latency value="0.000000"/>
      <DualHead value="Yes"/>
      <Offsets X="0.330000" Y="0.330000" Z="0.680000" X2="0.000000"
Y2="0.000000" Z2="0.000000"/>
      <MountAngle Pitch="0.000000" Roll="0.000000" Azimuth="0.000000"
Pitch2="0.000000" Roll2="0.000000" Azimuth2="0.000000"/>
     </TimeStamp>
   </SVPSensor>
   <WaterlineHeight>
     <TimeStamp value="2003-223 00:00:00">
      <Latency value="0.000000"/>
      <WaterLine value="0.000000"/>
      <ApplyFlag value="Yes"/>
```

```xml
        <StdDev Waterline="0.000000"/>
      </TimeStamp>
    </WaterlineHeight>
    <TPEConfiguration>
      <TimeStamp value="2003-223 00:00:00">
        <Comment value="ss intelmann"/>
        <Latency value="0.000000"/>
        <Offsets>
          <MRUtoTransducer X="0.326000" Y="0.146000" Z="0.398000" X2="0.000000"
Y2="0.000000" Z2="0.000000"/>
          <NavigationToTransducer X="1.189000" Y="-0.506000" Z="3.399000"
X2="0.000000" Y2="0.000000" Z2="0.000000"/>
          <Transducer Roll="0.000000" Roll2="0.000000"/>
          <Navigation Latency="0.000000"/>
        </Offsets>
        <StandardDeviation>
          <Motion Gyro="0.020000" HeavePercAmplitude="5.000000" Heave="0.050000"
Roll="0.020000" Pitch="0.020000" PitchStablized="0.000000"/>
          <Position Navigation="0.700000"/>
          <Timing Transducer="0.001000" Navigation="0.001000" Gyro="0.001000"
Heave="0.001000" Pitch="0.001000" Roll="0.001000"/>
          <SoundVelocity Measured="0.500000" Surface="0.500000"/>
          <Tide Measured="0.010000" Zoning="0.200000"/>
          <Offsets X="0.020000" Y="0.020000" Z="0.020000"/>
          <MRUAlignment Gyro="0.000000" Pitch="0.000000" Roll="0.000000"/>
          <Vessel Speed="0.030000" Loading="0.030000" Draft="0.050000"
DeltaDraft="0.010000"/>
        </StandardDeviation>
      </TimeStamp>
    </TPEConfiguration>
</HIPSVesselConfig>
```

Appendix 2. Bathymetry Surface

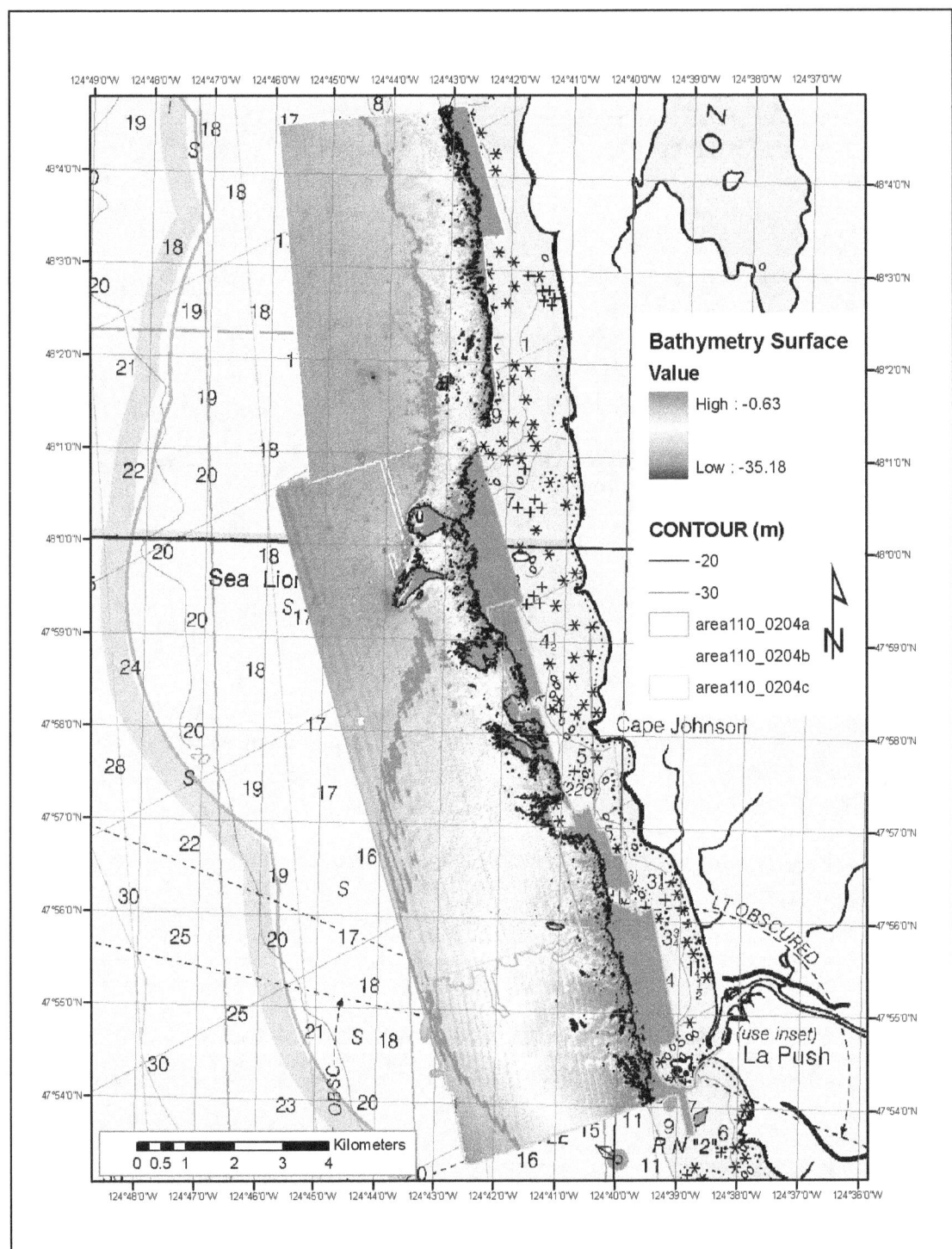

Appendix 2. Shaded relief surface generated from both 2002 and 2003 surveys overlain with -20 (black) and -30m (blue) contours.

Appendix 3. Backscatter Imagery

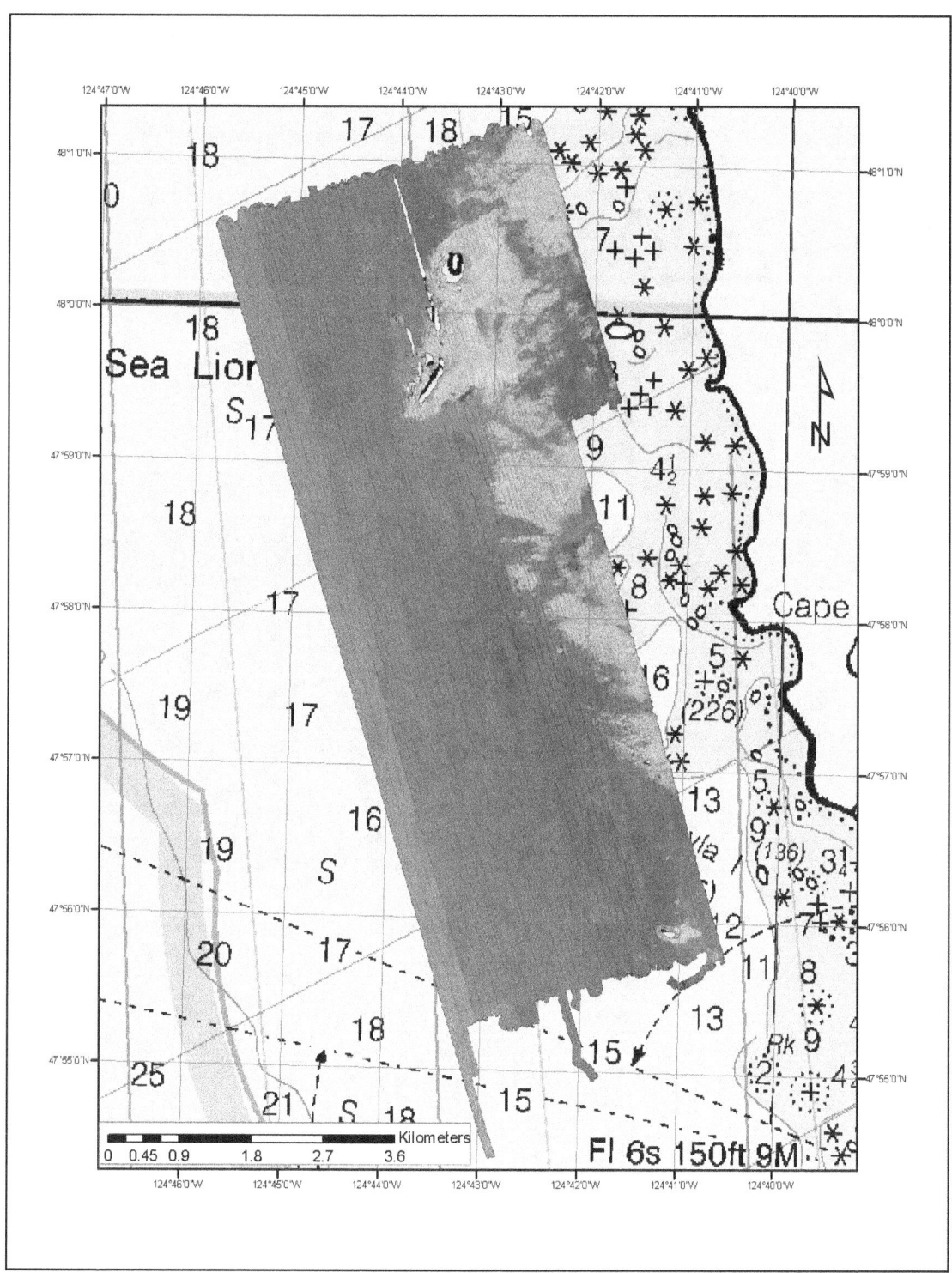

Appendix 3a. Backscatter mosaic of survey block 110_0204a. See Figure 1 for perspective of survey locations in relation to OCNMS boundary.

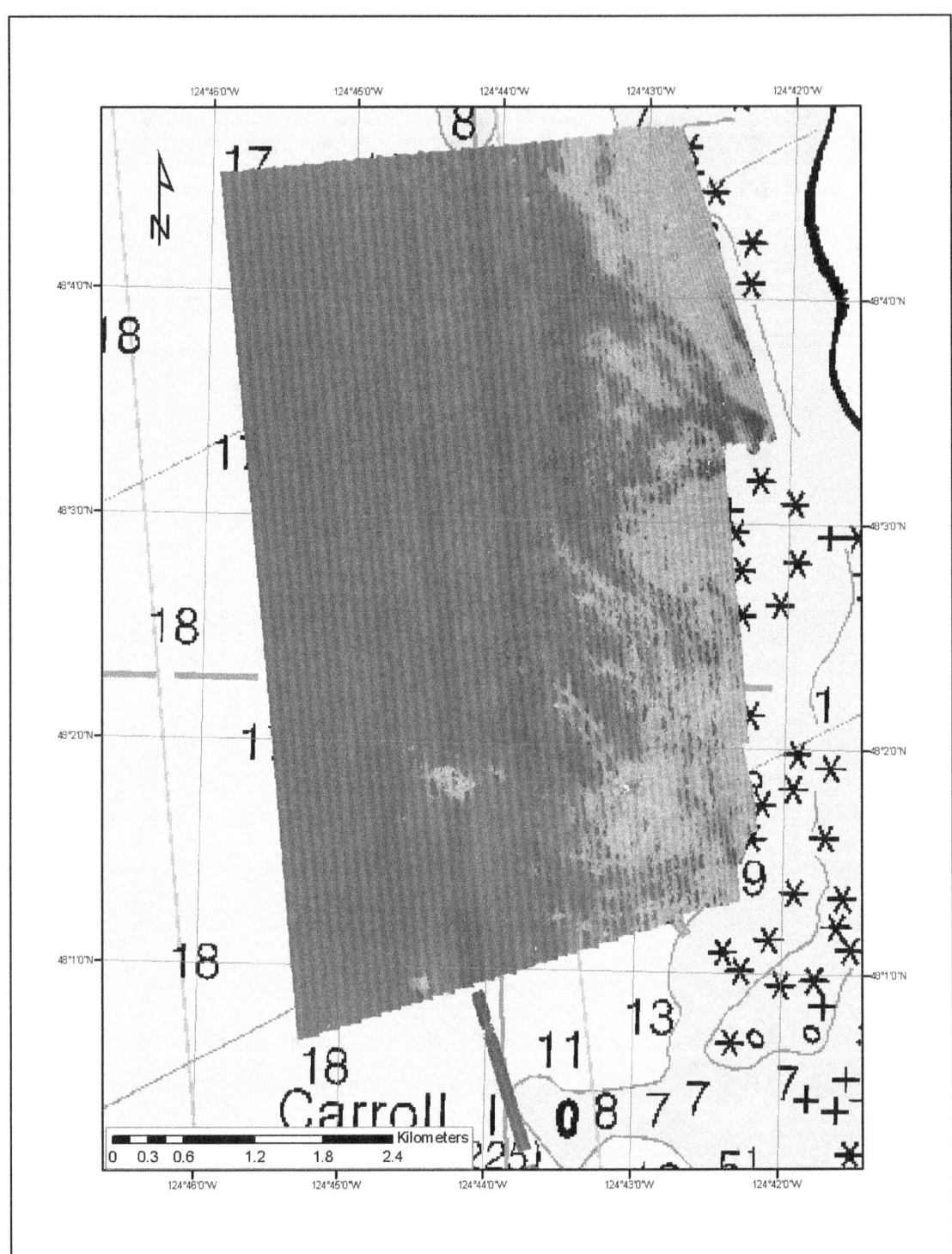

Appendix 3b. Backscatter mosaic of survey block 110_0204b. See Figure 1 for perspective of survey locations in relation to OCNMS boundary.

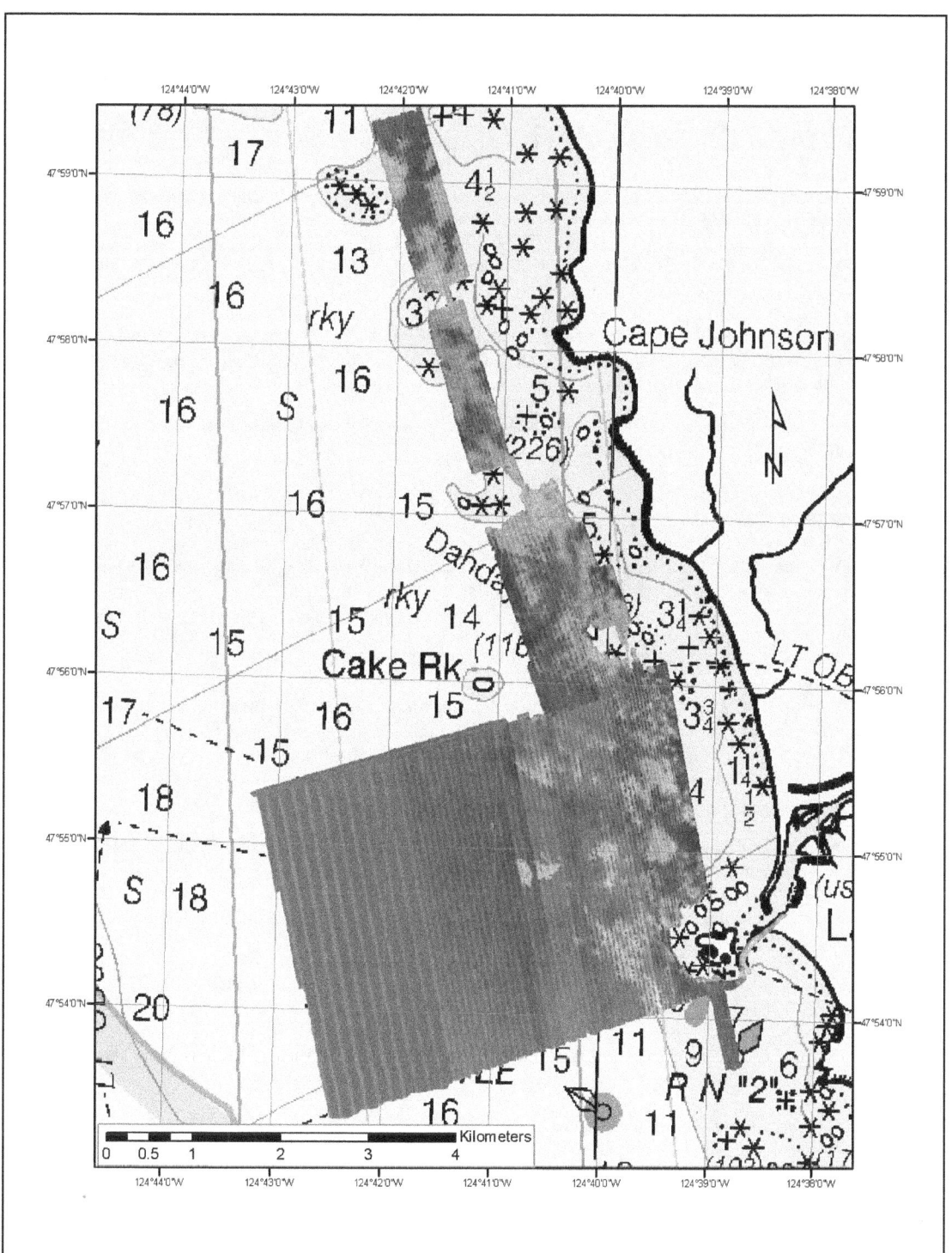

Appendix 3c. Backscatter mosaic of survey block 110_0204c. See Figure 1 for perspective of survey locations in relation to OCNMS boundary.

ONMS CONSERVATION SERIES PUBLICATIONS

To date, the following reports have been published in the Marine Sanctuaries Conservation Series. All publications are available on the National Marine Sanctuary Program website (http://www.sanctuaries.noaa.gov/).

Observations of Deep Coral and Sponge Assemblages in Olympic Coast National Marine Sanctuary, Washington. Cruise Report: NOAA Ship McArthur II Cruise AR06-06/07 (NMSP-07-04)

A Bioregional Classification of the Continental Shelf of Northeastern North America for Conservation Analysis and Planning Based on Representation (NMSP-07-03)

M/V *WELLWOOD* Coral Reef Restoration Monitoring Report Monitoring Events 2004-2006, Florida Keys National Marine Sanctuary, Monroe County, Florida (NMSP-07-02)

Survey report of NOAA Ship *McArthur II* cruises AR-04-04, AR-05-05 and AR-06-03: Habitat classification of side scan sonar imagery in support of deep-sea coral/sponge explorations at the Olympic Coast National Marine Sanctuary (NMSP-07-01)

2002 - 03 Florida Keys National Marine Sanctuary Science Report: An Ecosystem Report Card After Five Years of Marine Zoning (NMSP-06-12)

Habitat Mapping Effort at the Olympic Coast National Marine Sanctuary - Current Status and Future Needs (NMSP-06-11)

M/V *CONNECTED* Coral Reef Restoration Monitoring Report Monitoring Events 2004-2005 Florida Keys National Marine Sanctuary Monroe County, Florida (NMSP-06-010)

M/V *JACQUELYN L* Coral Reef Restoration Monitoring Report Monitoring Events 2004-2005 Florida Keys National Marine Sanctuary Monroe County, Florida (NMSP-06-09)

M/V *WAVE WALKER* Coral Reef Restoration Baseline Monitoring Report - 2004 Florida Keys National Marine Sanctuary Monroe County, Florida (NMSP-06-08)

Olympic Coast National Marine Sanctuary Habitat Mapping: Survey report and classification of side scan sonar data from surveys HMPR-114-2004-02 and HMPR-116-2005-01 (NMSP-06-07)

A Pilot Study of Hogfish (*Lachnolaimus maximus* Walbaum 1792) Movement in the Conch Reef Research Only Area (Northern Florida Keys) (NMSP-06-06)

Comments on Hydrographic and Topographic LIDAR Acquisition and Merging with Multibeam Sounding Data Acquired in the Olympic Coast National Marine Sanctuary (ONMS-06-05)

Conservation Science in NOAA's National Marine Sanctuaries: Description and Recent Accomplishments (ONMS-06-04)

Normalization and characterization of multibeam backscatter: Koitlah Point to Point of the Arches, Olympic Coast National Marine Sanctuary - Survey HMPR-115-2004-03 (ONMS-06-03)

Developing Alternatives for Optimal Representation of Seafloor Habitats and Associated Communities in Stellwagen Bank National Marine Sanctuary (ONMS-06-02)

Benthic Habitat Mapping in the Olympic Coast National Marine Sanctuary (ONMS-06-01)

Channel Islands Deep Water Monitoring Plan Development Workshop Report (ONMS-05-05)

Movement of yellowtail snapper (Ocyurus chrysurus Block 1790) and black grouper (Mycteroperca bonaci Poey 1860) in the northern Florida Keys National Marine Sanctuary as determined by acoustic telemetry (MSD-05-4)

The Impacts of Coastal Protection Structures in California's Monterey Bay National Marine Sanctuary (MSD-05-3)

An annotated bibliography of diet studies of fish of the southeast United States and Gray's Reef National Marine Sanctuary (MSD-05-2)

Noise Levels and Sources in the Stellwagen Bank National Marine Sanctuary and the St. Lawrence River Estuary (MSD-05-1)

Biogeographic Analysis of the Tortugas Ecological Reserve (MSD-04-1)

A Review of the Ecological Effectiveness of Subtidal Marine Reserves in Central California (MSD-04-2, MSD-04-3)

Pre-Construction Coral Survey of the M/V Wellwood Grounding Site (MSD-03-1)

Olympic Coast National Marine Sanctuary: Proceedings of the 1998 Research Workshop, Seattle, Washington (MSD-01-04)

Workshop on Marine Mammal Research & Monitoring in the National Marine Sanctuaries (MSD-01-03)

A Review of Marine Zones in the Monterey Bay National Marine Sanctuary (MSD-01-2)

Distribution and Sighting Frequency of Reef Fishes in the Florida Keys National Marine Sanctuary (MSD-01-1)

Flower Garden Banks National Marine Sanctuary: A Rapid Assessment of Coral, Fish, and Algae Using the AGRRA Protocol (MSD-00-3)

The Economic Contribution of Whalewatching to Regional Economies: Perspectives From Two National Marine Sanctuaries (MSD-00-2)

Olympic Coast National Marine Sanctuary Area to be Avoided Education and Monitoring Program (MSD-00-1)

Multi-species and Multi-interest Management: an Ecosystem Approach to Market Squid (*Loligo opalescens*) Harvest in California (MSD-99-1)

www.ingramcontent.com/pod-product-compliance
Lightning Source LLC
Chambersburg PA
CBHW080349290526
45791CB00009BA/2805